share with me

A Collection of Collaborations With a Four-Year-Old

by **Mica and Myla Hendricks**

thank you SO much...

...to my husband (my best friend), who has always, ALWAYS been supportive... and always encouraged my creativity and my confidence in my mom-abilities, no matter what. Even millions of miles away.

...to our family, friends, readers, backers, supporters, and complete strangers, who had total unwavering confidence that we could make this book, and fully supported us the entire way. You are ALL amazing!

...to our daughter Myla, who has taught me so much more than she will ever know. You are beautiful. You are smart. You are creative and lovely and kind. You are the most amazing person in the world, and I hope you *always* believe that.

Once upon a time, I thought of myself primarily as an artist.
I used to spend hours and hours, painting all day, or using any bit of free time I had to doodle in my sketchbook, which I carried with me at all times. It was always all about MY thoughts, MY feelings, MY ideas.

...And then we had a baby.

It's very strange going from a self-focused life, having all this free time to create for as long as you want, to suddenly using every ounce of energy to completely care for this other little person, with whom you're completely enthralled, but who needs you there every second of every minute of every day. That artistic, self-focused side doesn't go away right away; it just no longer has an outlet. As a new mom, I still had the urge to create, but no time or energy to do it.

So, when I wanted to draw, I stayed up VERY late. I sketched during that precious naptime where people tell you to "catch up on your sleep." And like most new moms, I was tired, but I think especially so since I was trying to exist in two separate ways...

...as an **ARTIST** and as a **MOM.**

As our daughter got older, we did typical kid crafts with her, like fingerpainting, papercutting and gluing, but I still kept my own art to myself, and drew and painted late at night, after she had gone to bed.

It wasn't until she was three that she started showing any interest in art, but when she did, she did it with a PASSION...something I could understand and relate to. I could watch her draw for hours, and was fascinated by her little brain at work.

But still, I kept my own art to myself....until she was four.

One day, while she was happily engrossed in her own marker drawings, I thought maybe I'd be able to get a little sketch time in of my own. I had just gotten a new tan-toned sketchbook, and was excited to try it out. So while she happily drew in her sketchbook, I quietly drew in mine, hoping to go unnoticed. And it was actually working! She was so focused on her own sketchbook that she didn't even notice me drawing in mine, and I was pretty proud of myself for being able to get some drawing in during the daytime for once.

Until she glanced over at me, instantly curious, and swooped in on me like a hawk.
"Is that a new sketchbook, Mama?" she said.
"Yes, honey, it is." ...Apparently, I'd taught her to recognize good art supplies.
"What are you drawing?" she asked me.
"Oh, just a head."

"OH. CAN I DRAW THE BODY?"

Oh dear. She wanted to draw in my NEW sketchbook.

"Uhh...Honey, you have your own sketchbook over there, with your own markers. WAY over there."

But then she looked me right in the eyes, and she used my own mommy-words on me. She said,

"MAMA, YOU HAVE TO SHARE. IF YOU DON'T SHARE, WE MIGHT HAVE TO TAKE IT AWAY."

Hmf. I wonder where she's heard that before.
Well, I was initially surprised that the lessons on sharing that my husband and I had tried so hard to instill in her had sunk in, and as much as I didn't WANT to share my sketchbook, I decided to go ahead and comply, to let her draw on it, chalk it up to a ruined page, and put my sketchbook up until after bedtime. I mean, that's what I get for getting it out in the first place, right?

Part of me thought, "This will be good for her. I want to show her that her creative ideas are just as valid as mine, and just as good as anyone else's."
But I didn't realize how good it would be for ME.

...And then she drew a dinosaur body on my lady's head.

She was so careful and meticulous with it. She wasn't nervous about it, she wasn't hesitant. She didn't worry about what I thought. She drew simply and confidently, just for the joy of drawing.

I was so fascinated by it that I flipped through my sketchbook, looking for more heads for her to draw on, because that's my favorite part...and usually only about as far as I get.

Pretty soon, she started ASKING me for heads to draw on. She'd wake up and say, "MAMA, DO YOU HAVE ANY HEADS FOR ME?"

I would draw some at night, and have them ready for her the next day. They were so much fun that I got my paints and markers out and started elaborating on them--hesitantly at first (it felt like treading on sacred ground)--trying to make the strange little doodles make sense by adding my own color, shading, and highlights.

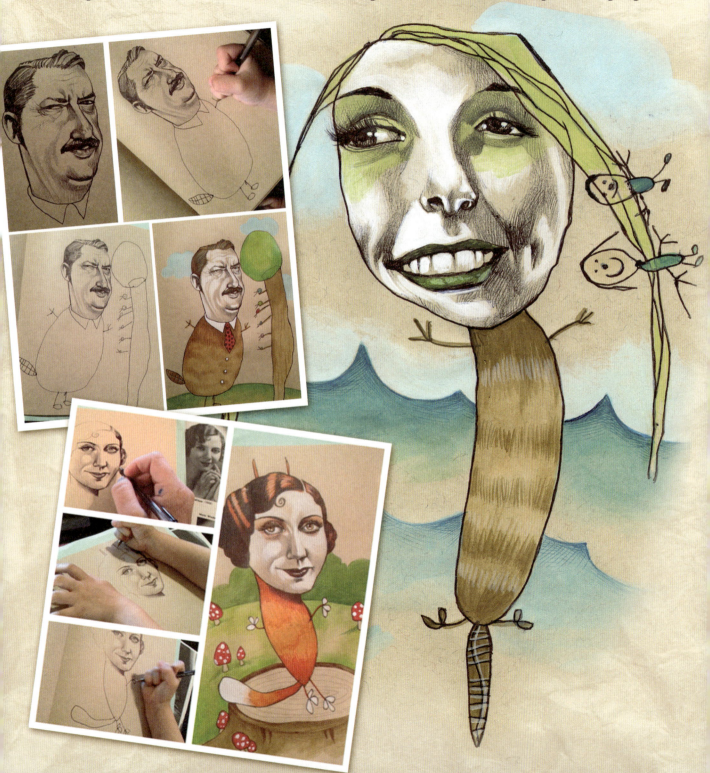

Also, I started realizing that as hard as I had been trying to keep my artistic life to myself, that it might actually be possible to make her a PART of it.

TO SHARE WITH HER THE THINGS THAT I LOVE.

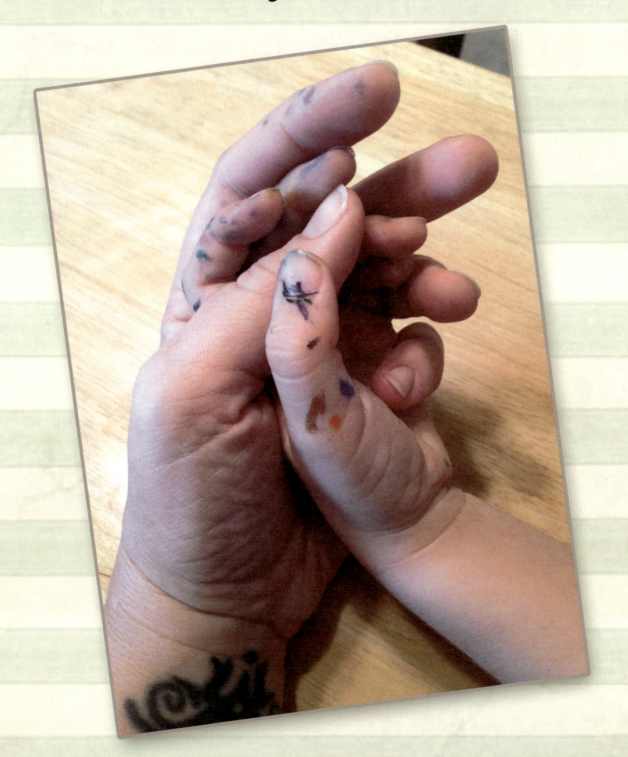

I think kids just really want to be a part of the things you love.

They want you to share it with them. And it doesn't have to be in art! It can be cooking, gaming, painting, sculpting, pottery, sports. Whatever makes your heart sing, SHARE it with them. If you don't know how to do something, consider learning something new WITH your kid. Not only will they grow from it, but so will you.

I've learned a lot from collaborating with our daughter. I've learned that my ideas about what should happen aren't always what NEED to happen. I've learned that sometimes when I let go of my own expectations a little and loosen up,

That's where the magic is.

And for awhile I get to see the world without fear of criticism or influence, or any real purpose at all—just the way she does: curious and playful and fun. And because I'm an adult, I have to KEEP relearning these lessons—but I GET to do that each and every time I spend time with our daughter.

Kids learn by watching you—so be a GOOD example to them, not by being perfect, but by sharing yourself. Experiment! Let things happen! Make mistakes, and help them handle it when THEY make mistakes. Follow your kid's lead every once in a while, without defining it so rigidly for her. Spend time listening to THEIR thoughts, THEIR ideas, THEIR opinions.

And don't hold anything so close to your heart that no one else can touch it.

How We Doodle

When our daughter first hovered over my sketchbook and asked to draw on one of my drawings, it was a lesson in letting go for me, and allowing her to be a part of something I have always been very passionate about.

First off, I love drawing from old black and white movie stills. For some reason, the far-off looks, the black and white imagery—I don't know why, but I could draw those all day. I like playing with the shapes, changing them a little, slightly altering them, and sort of abstracting the shading a bit. I work in ballpoint pen (because I love it, and I've used it over the years and years and years).

I'm always curious what she's going to draw. I can give her ideas, but she usually will decide what it's going to be AS she's drawing it. This was quite nerve-wracking for me in the beginning. It was HARD to let someone take something you worked on into a completely different direction. Sometimes I'd silently clench my teeth, do a mental gasp, and squint my eyes. But you know what? I swear, it all turns out fine in the end.

For this one, she drew this funky crescent-shaped body, and said, "She's a slug." Um. Okay. You turned her into a SLUG?! Some of the ones we had done were easy to collaborate on: a dinosaur, a bird, a dragon. But a SLUG? I kept any judgment to myself, and instead, decided to laugh with her about the lady with the slug body.

Thankfully, I'm always up for a challenge. And over time, doing these doodles with our daughter, I often think of my part as translating her ideas to make sense to grownups. It's a fun challenge to try to figure out a way to make her kid-doodle potentially exist in a two-dimensional environment.

For those curious as to who did what, the basic idea is always hers. She did the body, the antennae, the flower, and the sunshine on this one. Nowadays, she even gives me guidelines: "Don't forget, Mama—her wings should be BLUE." Or, "That's not a cracker. She's holding BREAD. Could you please make sure you color it to look like it?" In the end, we're both pretty surprised at the final result.

So after she decides what it's going to be and does her doodles, I do my part. I color in with markers (sometimes she helps). I used to use plain ol' Sharpies for base color, until I got a HUGE box set of my favorite brush-tip markers. So these days, when I get to this step, I use those instead, and I love love LOVE the color blending you can get with them. I add some white highlights with acrylic paint or sometimes watercolor.

Now's the fun part. How the heck to make this look like a slug, as opposed to a random, crescent-shaped doodle? I looked up some slug references, and did the best I could to fit those patterns into the shape she had drawn. I think the little "lip" underneath is what finally made it feel more "real."

I add a little more acrylic for the background. I added a little hopscotch grid to put her in some sort of context. I don't know why, but it just felt right. ...And because plain ol' grass gets boring. I did a little fine-tuning to bring the lines back with ballpoint pen. Often, I go back over the lines she and I both already made, to bring them out a little more.

And there you go! I call it "Slugs Need Hugs."

One time, playing outside, our daughter said it would be hard to try to give a slug a hug. When I finished this one, I felt a little bad for the little slug lady, trying to play hopscotch, while most likely being unable to perform the required "hopping." She seemed like someone in need of a hug.

As for any meaning or symbolism in turning a woman into a slug? There is none. AT ALL. I just like to draw faces. She just felt like drawing a slug. Simple as that.

As for my daughter's drawing skills? I understand that I'm her mother and while I can see all the beautiful, wonderful magic in the way she draws (and while her teachers have commented on how focused and detailed she is at drawing), I am the first to admit that maybe her drawings themselves aren't particularly masterful (I think they're amazing, and I could watch her draw all day). But, you know?—for that matter, neither are mine. Anyone focusing on that aspect is sort of missing the point.

So...what IS the point? To me, it's about enjoying the experience more than the end result. It's about helping your kids express themselves without limitations. It's about sharing your passion with someone else.

It's about taking that thing you love, placing it in someone else's hands, and trusting that everything will be okay.

Together, we have made some pretty lovely creatures.

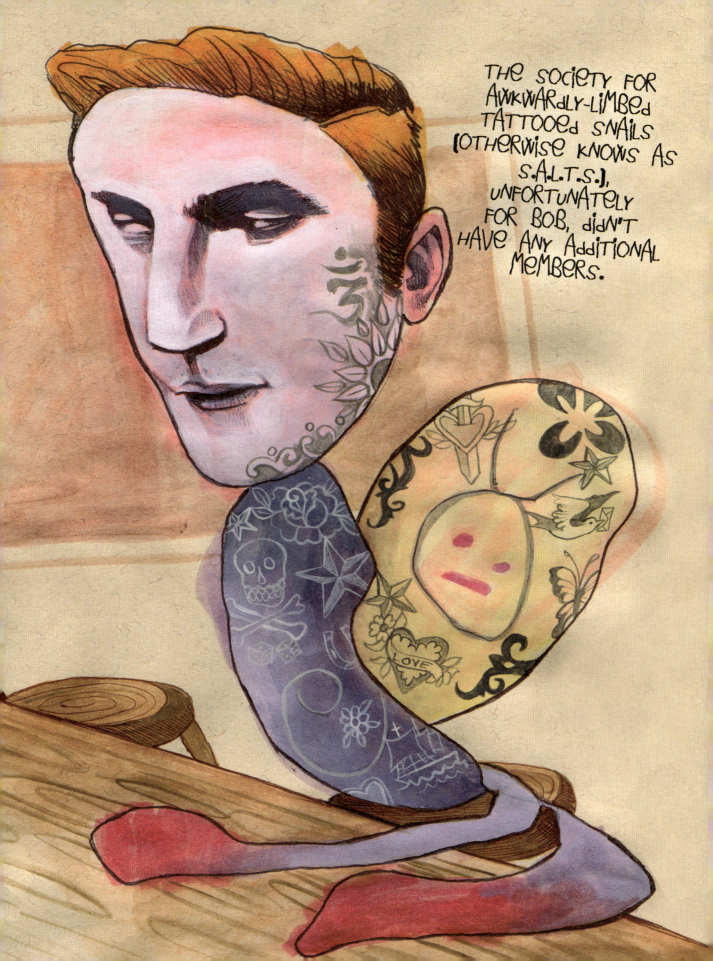

She may not have been able to hold a hair brush, but Harriet had always preferred her flippers for a good splash.

Marshall was so excited for his very first shift at the fire station that he slept in his helmet.

So if artists are inspired by the things around them, what is a four-year old inspired by?

LOTS OF THINGS.

Things all around them, things you teach them.
Things they see and hear and do.

Superheroes. Toys. Their favorite dolls.
Shows they've watched. Movies they've seen. Books you've read them.
Games they've played. Conversations they've had.
Places you go together.
A trip to the circus.   A trip to the grocery store.

Fill your kid's world with wonderful ideas, wonderful images, wonderful words.

IT WILL SHAPE THE WAY THEY SEE THE WORLD.

Sometimes, kids ask about things that are sort of over their age.
Maybe she sees something in a store, wonders what it is, but the story behind it is maybe not so age-appropriate.

Instead of shying away from it, answer the best way you can.

I've told her simplified versions of complex stories.
I never want her to feel strange or embarrassed for asking me an honest question.
Those are the things that will influence them and shape who they are.
Being open about little things makes it easier to be open about big things.
Because to a kid,

it's all big things.

this is not the end.

This is only the beginning!
Grab a marker. Grab a pen. Make a mess! Add on to this book. Draw and paint right in it.
Create your own book.
DON'T BE AFRAID TO MESS IT UP.
Make someone else—ANYONE else—a part of it.
Let someone else take the lead, and really listen to their ideas.
Take whatever you love the most and

SHARE WHAT MAKES YOU HAPPY.

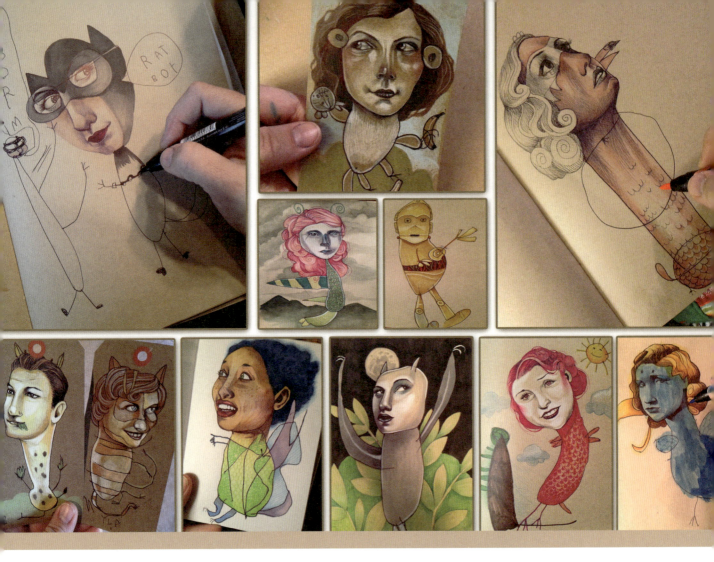

Copyright 2014 by Mica Hendricks. All rights reserved. In accordance with U.S. Copyright Act of 1976, the scanning, uploading, and electronic sharing of any part of this book without the permission of the artist/author is unlawful piracy and theft of the artist/author's intellectual property. If you would like to use material from the book (other than for review purposes), prior written permission must be obtained by contacting the artist at busymockingbird@gmail.com. Thank you for your support of the artist/author's rights.

Any trademarked, copyrighted, or otherwise legally protected characters depicted herein are used to show their influence on a child artist. All trademarked characters are the property of their respective owners, which are in no way associated with the artist/author. The use of a trademark of any third party does not signify or suggest endorsement, affiliation, or sponsorship of the artist/author or this book by any such third party.

Printed by The Avery Group at Shapco Printing, Minneapolis, MN (shapco.com/theaverygroup).
The artwork is a mixture of ballpoint pen drawings, marker, and watercolor with acrylic highlights, created in collaboration by illustrator Mica Angela Hendricks and her four-year-old daughter, Myla.
All text created by Mica Angela Hendricks.

busymockingbird.com
micaangela.com